THE END OF ABUSE

A Playreading in Three Parts

JOHN WOODS
with a foreword by Estela V. Welldon

OPEN GATE PRESS
LONDON

First published in 2001 by Open Gate Press
51 Achilles Road, London NW6 1DZ
Reprinted, with minor corrections, 2003

British Library Cataloguing-in-Publication Programme
A catalogue reference for this book is available from the
British Library.

ISBN: 1 871871 55 7

Printed and bound in Great Britain by PoD Ltd, London

John Woods is a psychotherapist working with children and adults. He lives with his wife and family in London. As well as this playreading, he has also published several articles on the practice of psychotherapy.

Estela V. Welldon is a consultant psychiatrist in psychotherapy at the Portman Clinic, London, and author of many publications, including *Mother, Madonna, Whore: the Idealisation and Denigration of Motherhood.*

Contents

Foreword

by Estela V. Welldon

Reading John Woods' play *The End of Abuse* was a very moving experience. Later on, when I saw it performed by a mixed group of therapists and professional actors, it became even more so. On that occasion I was privileged to be asked to lead the discussion and to offer some of my own insights about it. The play proved to be both powerful and true to life, even if at times quite painful to watch. Personally I felt deeply gratified that so much of my own clinical work with women in their dys/functioning as mothers had been represented in such a vivid way. Many aspects of our understanding of abuse seemed validated: for example, the concept of the three-generational process of perverse psychopathology.

Real life seemed to take over on the fifth floor of the
Tavistock Clinic on a Saturday afternoon in May 2001,
when the clinic was empty and no clinicians were 'per-
forming' in their own consulting rooms. This venue
added a sense of poignancy. Having worked just next
door, at the Portman Clinic, for thirty years, the play
evoked for me many scenes from my own professional
life. It was as though our patients had found their own
voice, and were teaching *us* in the Lecture Theatre.
Mary's response to her psychiatrist's inept question,
'Why did she have children', is just such a moment. In
an attempt to cover up her own inadequacy as a mother
she indignantly rebukes him by asking why did he
become a shrink. But to us she gives her real answer –
'I wanted to love someone' – and goes on to show how
it was not as easy as that. Her child's needs were as
unfulfilled as her own. In this way Mary repeats the daily
therapeutic insights that we get from young and immature
girls who feel so deprived of any solid and consistent
affection that they project their own longings onto a baby.
This baby represents different parts of themselves, but
most of all the desperate yearning for the love they never
had. Having babies may be the only way for some
women to communicate and express their own emotional
needs, which have not previously been either properly
addressed or recognised in themselves. And the trouble

is that this baby cannot then be seen as a separate entity, with its own needs that can, and must, be met by the parent.

When Mary asserts, 'I didn't want to give birth. I knew that's when the problems would begin', she is reflecting, in the clarity of her new-found freedom, upon the difference, so often overlooked, between the need to become pregnant and the demanding task of bringing up a child. Being pregnant gives a unique reassurance to some women about their extreme uncertainties at being of the female gender; it allays anxieties and even distaste for their own bodies and their reproductive functioning. She goes on to say, 'I was really frightened by the actual baby. More than by giving birth', thus making us look at the contradictory and somewhat unfair position which young girls with the most deprived and abused child-hoods have to face. That is, whereas they are able with their bodies to produce babies, they are unable with their minds and emotional resources to mother them. This discrepancy happens regardless of their conscious com-mitment to take proper care of their babies, since sud-denly and unexpectedly they feel unable to do so. They look for the support and care they need, but in many cases in this society, in this time and place, it cannot be found. Hence their despair and hopelessness are expres-sed either by inflicting harm on themselves or on their babies. 'No one showed me how to hold it', speaks to us who have in many cases failed to compensate for such a lack of parenting abilities.

Early motherhood acts as a substitute for their own emotional growth. John Bowlby described a pattern of 'compulsive caregiving'. The caregiver attributes to the cared for all the sadness and neediness she is unable to acknowledge in herself. It is as though the infant should provide the experience of being cared for that should have been given earlier. In this way the cared for person stands vicariously for the one who gives, or rather should have given, the care. According to Bowlby, this trait usually develops initially during childhood when children feel responsible for the welfare of their parents. These individuals are recognised as having what appears in the first instance to be a prolonged absence of conscious grieving, but they are actually suffering from unconscious chronic mourning. This is inextricably linked to extreme traumas associated with loss during early childhood, which are responsible for producing insecure attachments. Naturally, the relationship between mother and daughter is of fundamental importance for the girl's later capacity for motherhood. Predictably, we learn that Mary's mother was completely unable to give Mary a positive experience of being loved and cared for. Bowlby adds that 'should such a person become a parent there is danger of her becoming excessively possessive and protective, especially as a child grows older, and also of inverting the relationship.' Separation thus becomes intolerable, or if it is to happen it is brought about, as in this family's case, in destructive fashion.

Some women who have been victims of early sexual abuse may develop certain behavioural patterns, of a self-destructive nature, such as cutting, eating disorders, or drug addiction, which may escalate later on into sado-masochistic relationships with brutish men. On becoming mothers, they may develop a process of identification with the aggressor, in which they themselves, though they were early victims, may become victimisers of their own children. In my clinical experience, I have observed that these traits can also extend to intense ambivalence toward the child, resulting in periods of over-protectiveness followed by neglect and abuse. Hence the cycle of abuse crosses generations, through women's bodies, and continues in perpetual motion, regardless of social class or academic achievements.

The recognition of the cycle of abuse becomes even more painfully apparent when court reports are requested as evidence for life-making decisions regarding the future of the family, especially a mother and baby. I would like to bring in one such experience from a few years ago, when I was asked by a guardian *ad litem* to prepare a psychiatric report for a family court to decide about the future of a family in which all sorts of abuse had been disclosed.

During my long professional career and despite my own writings on clinical findings about perverted motherhood, I had been rather skilful in avoiding writing court reports or appearing in court as an expert witness. This easy state of affairs ended a few years ago when I was giving a lecture on female abusers and was confronted by a professional colleague about my alleged cowardice in refusing to lend the weight of my clinical experience in assessing parenting abilities. At that point I felt forced to 'grow up' before retirement, so I reluctantly agreed to be more co-operative and active in preparing court reports and giving evidence. But the complexity of the decisions concerning the future of parents and babies can make this an excruciatingly difficult process. Sometimes art has provided new meaning for me where there was none before. I was amazed to find one such, almost identical situation described in the play. Helen, the therapist is in search of some peace of mind while facing the enormous task her profession demands and expects of her. She goes, as I did myself, to an art gallery. She happens to see Rodin's sculpture *The Prodigal Son*. It appears to replicate her patient's appearance and conveys also his state of mind. I myself felt under extreme duress while writing a court report and it was then that I went to the Giacometti exhibition in London and in no time found myself unexpectedly in a state of distress by closely observing a sculpture of a woman with hands ready to hold a baby who is absent. The sculpture is framed in a rigid chair that may symbolise her having to be held or contained for her own safety or that of others because her child has been taken away from her, and is entitled: *Hands Holding the Void (the invisible object)*. This was not only a metaphor, so it seemed to me, but had become real, just like all those mothers we see whose babies have been or are about to be taken away. The woman's face in the sculpture appears superficially to be devoid of feelings, but when looked at in depth is a frozen image conveying such an unbearable psychic pain that its experience has to be blocked off. I wondered why on earth, when so many sculptures were on show at the exhibition, my eyes, heart, and senses took me to this particular piece, which was so relevant to my current work. I realised the impossibility of escaping from the experience of breaking up the most profound bonding – that of mother and baby. Perhaps I was too emotionally involved with it to allow myself to have a break, but this is the nature of this type of work. It holds you permanently in its grip; or is it that we need to be held in a way that is so unlike the mother who cannot hold?

But it is the last act of the play that gives us, the audience, and especially those clinicians who are group analysts, a sense of resolution. We move from Ruth's resistance, fury and her frustrated dependency triggered by the therapist's holiday (echoing as it does her abandonment by her mother all those years before), to the completion of the circle at the very end, when she announces she will return in September. Meantime we have heard the group analyst's ruminations about his involvement with her, his doubts and uncertainties in his role. He does this with courage, challenging himself as to whether he acted ethically or not. I feel that his confrontation with himself will mirror the experience of many colleagues, such is the degree of authenticity and pain he evokes. Perhaps the culture of group analysis enables therapists to process their stress more in relation to the social world, since they are not exclusively concerned with the 'intrapsychic' dimension of other psychodynamic treatments. Ruth enters a new dimension by owning and integrating both the abused/abuser contradictions and complementarities in her personality. She begins to understand the sibling incest in the context of parental negligence. One wonders if perhaps the earlier attempts at therapy for this family failed because in each case the patient was isolated with their therapist's individualistic model of 'vertical' relationships and was left alone without peer group support. The 'horizontal' peer relationships of the group provide an opportunity for an

open, liberating, therapeutic experience, with equals to
one's self, rather than having to struggle against those
seen as having power over the abused self.

There is much to learn from this insightful and accu-
rate play, not only about our patients, their difficult, and
at times, almost unbearable predicaments, and about the
underlying processes, but also about ourselves and how
we are in the course of our daily routine. Through this
work John makes all of us in the caring professions look
at our personal involvement and our emotional responses,
which are most often, of course, concealed from one
another and from ourselves. In a benign and compas-
sionate way he takes us to the imperative need for us all
to engage in constructive interaction with our colleagues,
not in competition. Essential requirements of supervision,
the modification of techniques, and changes in manage-
ment and treatment become obvious and undeniable.
Although it is painful to read and to watch, and could
even be seen as a masochistic act in itself, inflicted as it
was on a Saturday afternoon, it is also enjoyable, and at
times even humorous, especially when hearing familiar
voices that sound pompous and pedantic, as we try to
cover our feelings of helplessness, dealing with these
awful professional, and human situations. The discussion
which followed the play was intense, lively, at times
chaotic, but always riveting. We all, actors, clinicians and

audience were intensely moved and, though each from our own different perspectives, shared excitement, empathy and compassion. I highly recommend this play to everyone involved in understanding the various manifestations of child abuse.

Estela V. Welldon MD, DSc (Hon), FRCPsych
Consultant Psychiatrist in Psychotherapy,
The Portman Clinic, London

The End of Abuse

IN ORDER OF APPEARANCE

Mary Johnson *(early thirties)*
Dr Mark Hermann *(fifties)*
Sylvan Johnson *(late teens)*
Dr Helen Price *(late twenties)*
Anna (Helen's friend) *(forties)*
Ruth Johnson *(early thirties)*
John *(forties)*

PART I

MARY *is writing*

(She stops and looks at the audience.)

I dreamed I was drowning, fighting to get to the surface. My mother's body was in the way. I couldn't get to the air. I woke suffocating in the hot air of this flat. I hate this summer. I will bring in autumn.

(She resumes her writing, finishes, sorts through several pages and reads from the beginning.)

To Rob Ewart, social worker. You at least I thought I could trust.

But as you told me so many times, you've got a job to do.

I will never agree with it, in the end, what you lot have done.

With all the time I now have, in these weeks since it happened, I've been doing a lot of thinking; nothing else to do. It's so hot outside, I lie on the bed with the curtains drawn. I see the shadows on the wall of life going on outside.

I followed the cracks in the ceiling like it was the longest river in the world. Now finally I have some energy to write it all down so that you should know how I feel about what's happened. It's all jumbled up, as you know I hardly went to school,

– no excuses now,

And I won't say sorry to you for shouting.

I could have had more help, you know, not endless case conferences arguing over who said what to who, or therapy sessions picking over my past, but some real help, like say grandparents are supposed to do, take children for a holiday, or even a weekend, to give me a break. Or some money to help pay the bills, instead of the hours I have to spend in benefits offices. So I end up thinking it has really been unfair. I've had social workers, doctors, therapists, endless people telling me what to do, or how wrong I've been, but no Real Help. Ever. And I think I've tried my best. Drugs has always been brought up, but I've had that under control. Like-wise drink. OK, the children weren't looked after like they would be in the kind of family where there are two parents, plenty of money, grandparents – but I don't see why I have to be judged by those standards! To come in like that, with those child protection people, police! – to just arrive with no warning and take my children off like that to a 'place of safety'!

They were safe with me.

It shouldn't have been done that way.

And I would like, for the record, to set down the things I *have* done. I did give up heroin, did stay in every evening, did go to family guidance sessions, and did send them to school and nursery. But none of that was enough! The children are my life, Rob, and now my life has been taken away.

I've been trying to figure it all out the last few days, and work out why it has happened like this.

Lying here through these hot days, it's unnatural for this country, I think, to have sunshine.

I've been ransacking memories, searching for the reason, the start to where things went wrong. – No answer, – Maybe things were always wrong. One good thing I got from the family guidance centre, the few times I went, made me think about my childhood. Before I just thought I was bad and that was that. But I can't remember the face of my mother or my father. I've got no photo. Maybe I should have done that 'life story book' that someone tried with me when I was about 14, but I couldn't stick it. And when I wouldn't talk to that social worker, she looked so unhappy. After a while she just stopped visiting. What a bitch I must have been.

I've been trying to remember a time before, somewhere hidden behind all those rooms and houses I've been in. There is something I can almost remember, just see, or is it my imagination? I have a picture in my mind of some yellow flowered wallpaper, a sunlit time, and it was still, before the noise and mess of everything since. If I dig down deep enough, I've been thinking, if I go back far enough maybe I'll find the faces of my parents. But after this two weeks, or was it two months, I'm still down here at the bottom of a pit, with nothing much. I feel like I've been shipwrecked, but at least I feel calm now. The storm is over. I have some bits and pieces, a few not-so-bad memories.

Questions go round my mind. One doctor, can't remember his name, asked me why did I have children anyway – stupid question! – Why did he become a shrink? – Something to do. And what else was there for me to do? I wanted to love someone. I can't say that I loved their fathers. I slept with them because I needed someone, and they were around. They could give me drugs and I would feel OK, at least for a while. I can't remember which ones they were, which nights it was. I wasn't taking too much notice of things at the time. But then when I first felt something new in me, I was so pleased. I thought now my life could mean something. I stopped taking so much drugs. I felt better. I loved being big with baby in me. I felt like a great fruit, bulging with ripeness. I was strong, now at last I could do something. I could be somebody. I wanted to stay that way. I didn't want to give birth. I knew that that's when the problems would begin – I was frightened by that baby. More than by giving birth. Its arms and legs were everywhere. I couldn't hold it. No one showed me how to hold it. It was all slimy and wriggly, like an octopus with tentacles reaching for me. I felt it was going to suck me dry. I didn't want it. I wanted to kill it before it killed me, I can admit that now. I learned a bit how to cuddle it. Giving it a name helped I think. Sylvan, said Jake who I was living with at the time. Why Sylvan? I asked. It sounds mysterious and dark, he said, like you. And as it started to look at me and smile, I could love him. But it was difficult, he wouldn't sleep and wouldn't even be put down, nothing would satisfy him. It was him, I swear to God, who drove me back on drugs. I needed a break and how else could I get one? Who was going to give *me* a holiday?

– Then the next one and being big was over again all too soon. It felt a bit like some compensation that it was a girl, no extra bits like a boy, much more neat and – well, like me. It will be a little me, I thought at first, things will be better. And they'll keep each other company. But in fact it was worse. I could cope with two about half as well as I could with one. And then for some reason I found I would get more angry with Ruth than with Sylvan. I thought that being a girl, she should be good and more quiet, but instead her crying did my head in completely and I became terrified of being left alone with them. I could have killed either one of them, or both. I can admit it now, but how could I have said that then? Either to you or to Margaret. You would have taken them away. Wrapping them up tight worked a bit. I loved making them smooth, no bits sticking out. I used to hold them close if they were quiet, and imagine they were back inside, part of me again. I could hold them against me even though both of them were there, with no difference between them and me. Thinking about it now reminds me again of being pregnant. It was hot like it is now, I was swollen like a seed pod, about to burst. And when it did burst it was the end of me. And I can't do all that again. There's no point. I've been through it, at least it lasted a few years.

Time drags in this heat. No point in going out, where would I go? To meet someone? I've met all the people I want to. I used to fight against this feeling of pointlessness. When I was cutting myself. Before I had children. A cut used to keep me going. But I'm past that now. Cured of cutting. Cured of drugs, alcohol, men. Cured of motherhood. Cured of life! All I need now is a rest from it all. I'm still angry, I know, and that's my fault. I'm trying to get over it. If I can have a long rest I will be over it. If there were a switch in my arm to push and end my life, it would be so easy, but how to get rid of this body that hangs on me like a dead weight, a carcass, how to let it go.

(Pause)

I've been thinking about Janet and wondering how things might have been different for me if she'd stayed. It's a waste of time thinking over what might have been, but while I'm setting the record straight about some things, I want you to know why I never went back to see Margaret at the family guidance. It was her attitude to me and Janet. She and the other one whose name I can't remember were just so ready to judge, you could see it in their eyes. Lesbian. Pervert. They didn't need to say the words. I felt so betrayed, I'd said about that in my one-to-one session with Margaret. I told her because I was trying to explain how there was, or had been, some love in my life. She closed up soon as I said it and I just felt how critical she was. It was a mistake to tell her about Janet. Maybe I told her too soon. I've always dived into things too soon. I liked Margaret and I'm sorry I only saw her a few times. There were so many appointments I missed. I needed someone, but she seemed so tense and serious, I felt I always had to make her feel OK. She was silent and it seemed like she could never think of anything to say, anything ordinary. I think she might have been afraid of me. She always came out with these strange remarks, something about herself being the bad mother who goes away. I suppose I told her about Janet to show her there had been someone who I'd loved and who I was missing and that it wasn't Margaret. Perhaps also I was testing her out a bit to see if she'd be so predictably middle class. The following week she said something strange about how I was trying to make Janet into a sexy kind of mother. It was my way I think she said of trying to bring my mother back to life. I have been puzzling over that the past few days, but Janet was nothing like my mother and my feelings to Janet nothing like my feelings to my mother.

I don't remember my mother.

I remember – or was I told? – When I was four I woke up with her dead in the bed beside me from an overdose.

I don't have any feelings about her. Perhaps there is an emptiness and deadness in me, but Janet brought me to life. Being with Janet was nothing like . . . making love with Janet was nothing like the empty feeling I have when I think of my mother. As I tried to explain this to Margaret she started on about my feelings to her, saying that now she, Margaret, was the empty mother who died when I wasn't with her. I couldn't tell her that I didn't feel that way, certainly nothing sexual toward her. In the end, we couldn't agree about anything and I began to wonder who the hell I was going along for, her or me? How do I control the children, I asked her, how do I get them to behave a bit better, and stop them driving me mad? She said that they were the mad bits of myself that hates mother for going away.

I stopped going. I don't know, maybe I didn't understand properly what she was on about. It was over my head. I needed peace.

Janet was the first person to understand me, I suppose the only one. I couldn't understand why she came up and talked to me that first day in the park when my kids were playing. She was small, and smart with black clothes and short black hair. The kids loved her as well. She came back to the flat and after the kids went to bed she asked if she could take a shower. I was sitting in the kitchen when she came out in a towel and said, You're lovely with the kids. But there's something missing for you, isn't there?

When she reached out and touched my hair I burst into tears. I had no idea why. She leaned over and kissed my face, and the towel dropped. I had never seen how beautiful a body could be except in books, an art book I saw once. Her slim white body with small breasts was like a marble statue. She was more experienced than me, but her body was like a virgin's or a child's next to mine, so . . . used. I adored her, her smooth shoulders, long neck, I could have lain on her pearly breasts forever. But I knew it couldn't last long. Her green eyes looked past me sometimes, I was too possessive, she said. I felt so inferior. I heard about her clever friends, artists, dancers. I could never explain what I really felt, which was that I wanted to *be* her, not this shabby single mum whose figure had gone. She was everything I wasn't and could never be. I couldn't understand why someone like her would even want to be with me. But she was loving and gentle. She smiled on me as I told her I've never felt this way.

Don't ask too much, she said.

No wonder it didn't last. I was so hungry for her. I could never feel that way about a man. She said that at the end she was sorry. I couldn't stop crying. She said, I can't live your life for you.

I'm not sorry about what happened because I had something, short as it was. I had a glimpse of what a real love could be. I had so little before. I was depressed, I suppose, for a long while after, maybe ever since. For a time I thought about her all the time, and then she became like a nothingness in my mind, an empty hole. The children forced me to keep going, but it was difficult to be at all positive for them. Perhaps it was selfish of me, but I was in the grip of something. I couldn't help it, the light had gone out of my life. I dragged myself through each day. Even if the kids were happy and I was playing with them, the thought was always there, when is there going to be someone for me?

So when Ron came along, I just felt that here was someone who might look after me for a change. He wasn't going to abuse me, he wasn't into drugs and he loved the kids. When I heard in the case conference that he had convictions I went mad. Offences against children! I couldn't help myself, maybe I shouldn't have screamed like that. I didn't know who to scream at first, him for keeping it secret, you lot for sitting there in judgement, the kids for what they maybe were not saying. But they never said he touched them, did they? And I know they would, they would have told me. The trouble is, I can say it now, I can understand how they love the smooth white body, stroking, touching them, but actual sex, no. Then after that, you were all just looking for a reason to take them into care. Ron had gone, I wasn't allowed to see him, suddenly nothing. After all the social workers coming and going, questions, questions to the kids, to me, suddenly nothing. I had to pick up the pieces, the kids in a state, demanding, whining, where was Ron, they asked. The weeks passed and it felt like we were forgotten. And I let my guard slip. I went out. Left the kids one evening, came back late, and there you were, getting ready to take them away. You had moved in. I was punished finally. I had to wait all through that weekend for the case conference on Monday and then it was cancelled, only another few days they said so that we can study the reports. And then it was 'a . . . cumulation of risk factors', you said. Some specialist report had come through two months after one of those interviews and it said that 'on balance of probablies . . . probables?' . . . or something like that, the children were at 'risk of abuse'. So there was no one thing for me to argue against. No one was accusing me of anything in particular. The care order was supposed to be temporary, but it felt like I would never get them back. I came out of the meeting and walked for miles and miles, not knowing where I was going. Eventually I was so tired I got on a train without a ticket, got away with it that time, and back to the empty place I wanted so much not to be in. Nowhere else to go.

The last two weeks – I've been letting the time pass. Going out to the telephone, ringing your office ten times before I could get through, to be told you were on leave. No one else could tell me where the children were placed, you'd get back to me as soon as possible and so on and so forth. Perhaps they're better off with someone who can cope, someone who isn't depressed. If I met them on one of the contact visits you keep on about, I couldn't stop myself wanting them to be difficult and badly behaved, not to love their foster parents, but be angry and come back to me! But that wouldn't help them. It would be better if they were happy where they were. Perhaps I shouldn't see them at all, maybe they should make the break from me.

I stopped getting food, stopped going out, stopped everything. This must be the longest suicide note ever. It's the longest thing I have ever written. I tried to get everything down for myself, to be able to see it written out in front of me. I wonder what it will be like to see the water flood red around me when I cut my wrists.

It should be kind of beautiful, but maybe just a mess. If there were a way of quietly just leaving the world and shutting the door, I would have done it, but this body is such a burden, a sack of bones and blood and shit, it has to be thrown down somewhere and someone has the job of clearing it up. I'm sorry it has to be you.

Please tell the children I was ill. And tell them I was sorry I couldn't say goodbye.

(She signs the letter)

Signed, Mary Johnson

(Blackout)

PART II

DR HERMANN

Welcome to our new staff member, Helen Price! And we have a case that I think is quite suitable for you to . . . er, cut your teeth on, as it were.

(Addresses audience as if in a clinic meeting.)

The young man in question, Sylvan Johnson, nineteen years old, was referred to us by the Social Services Department after a Court Order for treatment . . ..

(He consults his notes on and off.)

. . . in connection with sexual offences against his half-sister aged 13. He was at that point 16. He has already completed one year of compulsory treatment in a Cognitive Behavioural Group Therapy Programme 'designed to correct his sexually deviant thought patterns and behaviour'. We are informed by the agency that provided the CBT that the group was undermined by Sylvan. The group therapists state in their report that 'his compliance in treatment was superficial, with little real engagement and a barely concealed contempt for the group'. Individual psychodynamic treatment was recommended because Sylvan showed

(He reads.)

'an occasional desire to talk about feelings, though he quickly withdraws when interest is shown'.

(He looks up.)

So, as usual, we get called in when all else fails!

(He flicks through file.)

Family background . . . parents split up before he was born, probably a casual relationship. Sylvan was taken into care aged four . . . neglect . . . mother committed suicide . . . Maternal grandmother too, it seems . . . First foster placement broke down after 18 months . . . soiling and temper tantrums. After some months in a children's home, another fostering placement attempted . . . Sylvan's behaviour deteriorating . . . it seemed he was being sexually abused and bullied in this placement . . . perpetrator a teenage boy who was also being fostered . . .

Sylvan reunited with his sister and placed in a children's home, but concern as their relationship was said to be 'overclose and sexualised' . . . They were separated. Then a series of placements, each one breaking down until at 13 he was placed in a therapeutic community . . . had to leave at 16 when funding was withdrawn by the local authority. And it seems that it was at this point that he sought out his sister and stayed with her in her placement. She admitted that there had been sexual relations . . . there was a supervision order . . . treatment recommended. Currently in a hostel with little social work supervision . . . on benefits . . . no work or education.

(He looks up from the notes.)

It is clear from all this that there has been severe disruption of attachments throughout this young man's life. No security or stability whatsoever. His relationships have been shot through with abuse and destructiveness. If we are to offer treatment then he should be in a safe and supervised environment. Can the Social Services provide this? Group therapy failed to engage with his emotional needs, hardly surprising, really. Individual psychotherapy could perhaps get to grips with the depth of his difficulties and meet the experience of deprivation. But

(to Helen)

we have to ask ourselves, is there enough ego strength in this patient to tolerate being in touch with his inner pain? These are some of the difficult questions that I had in mind when I met him myself . . .

I rather liked him.

(He refers occasionally to notes.)

He acknowledged that he was under some duress from the social worker, but said that he welcomed the opportunity to talk privately because there were a lot of thoughts and feelings he wished to understand. He said that he 'had sex', as he put it, with his half-sister Ruth because she reminded him of Sadie, a girl he had met in a children's home when he was five or six years old. Sadie was a bit older, nine or ten, and took him into her bed. It seems from his description that the affection he craved was from this point on inextricably bound up with erotic impulses. We know little about this Sadie, but it seems that sexualised behaviour was pretty rife in the children's home. Sylvan had been treated violently and abusively in the previous foster placement, and in the arms of this older girl he felt a warmth and comfort that must have seemed bliss by comparison. Having learned that this was the way to find love, he was bound to see the sister, from whom he had been separated for so long, in the same way. He agreed with me that sexual behaviour with a sister was inappropriate. He was in touch with feelings of loss and sadness about his life though also seemed cut off and inaccessible at times. He had a reasonable rapport with me, and I felt quite optimistic about treatment. This was defensive, of course, because I felt a distinct reserve from him, a watchfulness typical of children with avoidant–attachment features. Hostility was not far from the surface, and I think that acting out and suicidal behaviour is quite possible. However, he is obviously in need of help and in view of the fact that he could express some of these feelings it seemed to me that there was a chance that he could be helped by psychotherapy.

Ideally, of course we would provide intensive psychotherapy but due to our funding difficulties, and the Trust's lack of confidence in our work, we have only once-a-week treatment possible.

(He turns to Helen)

Well, Helen, what do you think? Want to give it a go?

(Blackout)

SYLVAN *(sitting at desk, he reads from his letter)*

Dear Helen, I decided to call you Helen, I hope you don't mind. You did introduce yourself as Dr Price, shrinks do that I know, but you seemed less distant than the others I have met. Perhaps you conform because it is less hassle. If only I could learn to do the same! I came to see you a few times, as Martin said I should. Social workers don't seem to mind their first names being used. How friendly they are! Even if they are just about to flush you down the toilet, and send you to some god-awful children's home to get shouted at and abused. They smile and smile . . .
But I know that you tried to be straight with me. I could have spoken to you. I don't want you to think that it was your fault I stayed away. When I was silent you said that I was afraid of being rejected. Yes of course that was true, but you know, it wouldn't be a shock, I'm pretty used to being rejected and I don't want your pity, I spit on that.

Not that I think you do pity me, no, I felt that you could understand me and you know I want to change, and be different, but something happened and I just felt I couldn't do it,

I couldn't do it.

I don't know why. I can't really understand it myself. Maybe it was that I didn't want to spoil things with you. You seemed a really good person, and if we got going, I mean if I started telling you everything, then I would begin to hate you for it.

So I missed a few times. And then it became more and more difficult to come back. I got your letters to the hostel, and I liked getting them, even though they were rather the same:

'I was sorry not to see you for your appointment' . . .

'The next appointment is . . . etc.'

They were a little more exciting than the social security letters, and so forth. You kept sending me appointments but I dis-appointed you.

But since you did write to me, I thought I should reply.

I will not be coming back. I cannot do psychotherapy. Yes. I know that the Clinic has such a great reputation, Martin told me so many times how lucky I was to be getting the best. There is just something about it I cannot do. Being passed around from doctor to doctor gets on my nerves, not that I wanted to see that other bloke with the foreign sounding name again. He was a bit up himself. I want to talk to you. So can I write instead?

I was told to see you, and OK, it put me off to start with. You didn't seem pleased at my saying you were like my foster mum, Doris. OK, I thought you were like her. I meant that I liked you like I liked her. But because you seemed unhappy about that I didn't go on with the story, you see, what happened is what always happens – when I keep talking, things go wrong. She was a nice lady, and when I went to stay with her, it was a shame, I wasn't what she expected – or wanted. She threw me out – for looking in her cupboard. One day after a smoke, desperate for something to eat, I went into her cupboard over the telly, found nothing. Later on she came up and said there was a smudge on the television. The cupboard had been opened!

How can I trust you again? she said, Why did you go into that cupboard? It makes me glad I never had children of my own. I'm sorry, but you cannot stay here any more if I can't trust you.

I could say What a bitch, but then, it was her house and she can have who she wants. Pretty soon it would have been clear I wasn't what she wants. So it was back to the children's homes, and so on.

With her garden gnome husband, let Doris live her little existence unperturbed.

You could never be the 'good mother', you said. What

you don't understand about me though is that I want no
kind of 'good mother'. I do need someone to talk to, and
for more than an hour a week!

To tell you everything that has happened to me, the
places I've been, the things I've seen, would take too
long. I have a lot of time, ironically. Time weighs heavy,
like iron, on me. Maybe you wouldn't bother to read it,
maybe you won't read this, perhaps you don't have time.
Does it fly for you? In any case I will send this, at least
I will have said something.

Yours truly, Sylvan.

(Blackout)

HELEN *(reads from her letter.)*

Dear Sylvan, Thank you for your letter. It was helpful
for me to hear something of what has been going on for
you. I am sorry that you feel unable to continue with
psychotherapy. You were strongly recommended to do
this, though no one can force you. It needs time for us
to see how we could work together. You came to two
sessions only and I wonder if you feel you did give it
enough time. You say that you want to speak to someone
and you seem to expect it will be easy. Perhaps it can't
be easy.

The sessions you missed were just before the summer break. Could this be because you were going to find it difficult to say goodbye for four weeks?

It seems from your letter that you did find our conversations useful and perhaps of some importance to you, even though you sometimes said little. Your letter tells me that you do want to keep a link between us and that we might yet do some work together. I remind you therefore that the first appointment back is on Monday September 4th at 11.00 a.m. and I hope to see you then.

Yours sincerely, Helen Price

(Blackout)

DR HERMANN *(reads from his memo.)*

Dear Helen, re Sylvan Johnson. Thank you for sending me the latest of this patient's letters to you and a copy of your reply. It seems that I must put in writing some of what we discussed in the clinic meeting before going on holiday tomorrow.

I have to say that I would not have written back to him in that way. You see, from the first point he insists on the familiarity of first names and in doing so he attacks the therapy. He is saying in effect, you are not my therapist, but the same as me. He attacks the boundary between therapist and patient. This is because he cannot stand the transference that would exist for him in relation to you. You are, in his mind, the mother who allowed the abuse, abandoned him, and against whom he is so angry that it justifies all the hostility in his relationships. He expresses this also by bringing in a more superficial, though entirely consistent, transference of the aunt who rejected him. This material also shows the erotic element; he wants to get into your cupboard, steal anything good you may have and leave his mark. His contempt for the 'garden gnome' husband shows the lack of any oedipal father figure that would help him contain his incestuous desires for mother. His inability to tolerate boundaries is of course what led to his offending behaviour. For him to work on any of this would require the first step of accepting some limits to his desires, and a capacity to tolerate the pain of separation. But, as we discussed when you presented this case at the clinical meeting, his resentment and defensiveness serve to protect him from his fear of breakdown. There is an ego-ideal of himself as a sensitive and intelligent person which he tries to mobilise in relation to you but it is sexualised in a perverse way that means he would re-enact the sado-masochistic relationship with his internal mother. This is why it is most important not to get drawn into an acting out of anything that he would perceive as a gratifying relationship. My apologies for having gone on at such length, but if he fails to attend for the appointment in September then his treatment is terminated. After writing to the referrer, we close the case.

Signed, Mark Hermann, Consultant Psychotherapist.

(Blackout)

HELEN

Dear Anna, The job I so much wanted in this clinic, so famous and highly regarded, has gone sour so quickly. I would appreciate some professional advice as well the support of a friend. It's about my first psychotherapy case, a 17-year-old convicted of sexually assaulting his 13-year-old half-sister. Basically it has been a disaster. He came twice, said very little, and missed the last sessions before the summer break. He has written saying he won't come back. All that would be par for the course; adolescents frequently drop out and none more so than offenders. But he has also told me about those feelings that actually make it impossible for him to stay in the sessions. I replied, and it is this which puts me in a real quandary now. Mark Hermann is not happy with this letter writing. He feels the patient is acting out an erotic and masochistic transference. Maybe he is right, but I just

feel that it is a way of keeping in touch with a very vulnerable young man who needs a lot of help. If he is kept
in contact there is at least a chance that he will return to
therapy. But as a new arrival I cannot go against the consultant. In the clinical meeting everyone thought I was
being soft and manipulated by the patient. When I argued
against this they saw me as colluding with the psychopathology, unable to cope with his hostility. Excuses were
made for me on account of my lack of experience! I was
absolutely furious at being patronised in that way! I keep
telling myself I must try to understand why I'm being
polarised against the rest of the clinic staff like this.
They're so damned precious! Perhaps Sylvan *is* getting
under my skin in some way. The situation is stirring up
such bad feeling. Mark Hermann says I have become
over-involved. Have I been seduced by the patient, as he
says? I need your help.

Love, Helen

(Blackout)

SYLVAN

Dear Helen, In Russia a 6-year-old boy was found having
lived with wild dogs for more than two years. He had
run away from home. The dogs found him shelter and
brought food. He said he had been happier with the dogs

than with the parents who abused him. The newspaper reporter seemed amazed. I find it completely believable. Stoned in the public library, I have time to reflect on these things.

(Pause)

Thanks for writing. It made me think that someone is willing to listen and see me as a person. People see only the offence, they hear 'indecent assault against a minor', the history of 'criminal damage, burglary, theft, illegal possession of drugs', and that's it, I'm condemned straight away. I don't stand a chance. I know people who have done a lot worse than I have. My crime has been getting caught. And I know I should come back but I don't know if I can. Because when I'm with you, anything I say comes out wrong. Maybe I should be more patient, but . . . The trouble is that by the time we've started to get somewhere, it's time to go. And then it all feels so pointless. It's frustrating because I do want to keep contact. I want this to be pure. Not like everything else.

I've been trying my hand at some poetry.

The forests of Europe
Stuffed with corpses
Black earth and brown leaves

Soon mulch the pale skin of the dead
While in the warm wet parks after Sunday lunch
Londoners trudge in the shit-rich mud.

What do you think? Do you like it? I find that given time I can weigh each word and put it sometimes in what feels like exactly the right price (oh, I meant to write place). That must mean something!

I'm not going to say sorry that I didn't come back to the first appointment. I was going to be there, but I only just got myself out of hospital, the day before. They said I should stay but I know it was only in order to be nailed (in the nicest possible way) by Martin who bustles in like a saviour with his earnest face that says, 'look what a mess you're in again! . . . When are you going to realise how much you need me?'

I already had the visit from the psychiatrist college boy. He assumes it was a suicide attempt but could not quite say so. But I want you to know that I wasn't intending to kill myself. When I reach that point, I tell you, I'll do it properly. Actually the prospect of everyone's so-called concern would be enough to hasten me toward the light at the end of the tunnel. If it's there. I simply took too much drug, got completely fucked up . . . oh, I mean, felt really ill and turned myself in. The acid was the one that did it, and I was trying to get down with some smack and then some sleeping pills. Maybe the acid was bad, mixed with methedrine, something like that. I was getting too high. Even a smoke wasn't helping, making me feel more strung out. Some E would have been good, but there wasn't any around. I felt pushed out of existence. For a long while I felt that my body had no depth, it was about half an inch thick and I was walking around this enormous fish tank. At times I'd forgotten that I had taken anything at all. It was as though I'd just been born, or come from nowhere into this state. I was too high, couldn't remember my name, though I had a dim notion of something about a previous life and a vague memory of who I'd been before this. The spaces around me were so empty I felt I had to keep walking in order to reach the end of things, a place to rest, a place I could just be. I was walking 'down a street', or was it 'up a street'? I looked back and it was downhill. I looked forward and it was downhill. If I walked on I was still at the top of a hill. The road glistened as it stretched down behind and in front. I kept on walking to see if the top of the hill would always be where I was. Can this be real, I thought. I said to myself that I was at the top of the world. Always. Where I am, is the top of the world. If I'm not there then there is nothing. Now that I think about it, it's obvious but I suppose at the time it seemed that I had the power to end the universe because I was truly at the centre. So I was wondering whether everyone really *deserved* to die. I had my reasons for certain people to be terminated of course, but there were some innocent parties somewhere, of that I could be sure. After all, *you've* done nothing against me. I thought of this as I walked along and it reassured me.

Cars distracted me. I tried to ignore them. Walls of gardens in the darkening light seemed more solid than usual and I saw geometric patterns of leaves and branches reaching toward me, poking over, trying to get out from behind that wall. I can't tell you how everything looked so clear, never seen before. It wasn't just that things looked different, I realised I had never seen anything before. Now that I've come down I realise why this was so, it was that I'd never understood the meaning of anything. Things were flat before because they had no meaning. Now I understood that these walls had been built to keep life in, or out, and life yearned to be free, pushed its way over the wall, through the concrete, could pull down bridges, and would never be kept out. The plants were saying this to me, that they'd be held back only for a time. They will outlast us! Thick fingers, but carrying complex and delicate networks, beckoned to me out of the dark, clambering over, wanting to break out from behind their prison walls and be free. But I was wondering why speak to me? Were all living things on earth in prison? What was I supposed to do about it?

Cars were distracting. As they approached they seemed to take flight and somehow landed perfectly normally only a few yards in front of me. I pressed on. Cars, after all, are completely incomprehensible, if you're from another time. I thought about what I was, not who, not that individual who had evolved a mishmash of received and predictable ideas about his place in the accepted order of things, the person I used to believe I was, rather I wanted to know *what was I?* An animal of some kind, it seemed clear. I'd been sent for some reason yet to be discovered into this physical shape. And soon I saw similar creatures, walking about in front of me. Is this what humans are? I asked myself. They seemed oblivious to the hurtling tons of metal flying above their head. I noticed one standing by the road, teeth protruding from under the skin of the face with cheekbones and temples protecting the eyes, darting from side to side, on the watch from danger, was it hunter or prey? The tall thin body was concealed for the most part under soft material, but its claws were left naked at the end of the arms and its lower pointed hooves were encased in black shiny coverings. I could see the whole now was a reptile whose teeth, claws and scaly hide were cleverly hidden under a soft exterior. It did not appear to be aware of me so I avoided eye contact and shifted myself out of its way. I had no particular destination, I kept on going. The town was full of them, eyes everywhere, predatory and fearful. Suddenly I could feel all their thoughts, their aims and intentions, wanting to get here, waiting to get in there, getting off with this one, getting away from that one. No-one seemed to be able to see it all except me. I felt very alone. I thought there must be someone else like me. But I was being approached by one of the creatures and he looked familiar, like someone I'd known before a terrible transformation. Was it a cancer that turned the skin into a hard shell? Did the inner organs become like mechanical parts? It was speaking to me. I was trying to recall the previous existence out of which I might put together what to say. But the eyes pierced mine and saw straight into my brain and it burned. – 'Where were you last night? Where did you get the money to score?'

Where *did* I get the money to score? Where *was* I the night before? I was letting Bill, the rich old queer, suck me off for fifty pounds. His drug, my drug, what's the difference? What do you put in your mouth? Sex for money is not so uncommon. Everybody uses sex as a trade-off one way or another.

(Pause)

Read this, if you've got this far, and think what you like. Give up on me and it doesn't matter, I'm not there when you read it, I don't have to see your reaction. I know those creatures on the street are the mirror images of myself. Acid has that way of showing the truth. I always think afterwards I won't do this again. He is a disgusting old man but what else to do? Get fucked by social security standing in line all day? Or fuck old Bill for half an hour, at least I get my money quicker, get the drugs and pain soothed. Then the long hours in my room pass by bearably.

I'm writing this in the library, a nice place to be, cool in these oven-hot days. You can read and you can stay here all day.

I don't have to live with dogs.

Yours, Sylvan

(Blackout)

HELEN

. . . and so he pointed out, 'there is no indication what-soever that this patient is motivated to work in therapy of any kind'. He accepts that Sylvan needs help, of course, but it sometimes seems from discussions that people are quite happy that he is not going to accept it. In the clinic meeting the letters were discussed again. I tried to put forward my view of his isolation which has produced a very negative development. Mark said that Sylvan is in a downward spiral, a malignant regression in fact, and part of it, he said, is the relationship with me. My reading his letters was an acting out of the counter-transference. There were knowing nods around the room. And his fantasy that I am so interested in him causes further deterioration. I have come to represent, so they said, 'the sexualised and forbidden mother whom he imagines he can join in death'. In this way, it was said, he continues to derive perverse pleasure from acting out sexually, because I am there in his mind as someone he can penetrate with his perverse letters. By this means he denies his self-destructiveness and glorifies his ability to distort reality with drugs. The recent admission to hospital they all felt was a certain sign of suicide. I was seen as colluding in all this and the meeting became a very unpleasant experience. I pointed out that a traumatised person does find it difficult to let anyone be close. Writing is his way of keeping contact. I said that he is also trying to reclaim a mind when he writes, and thinks, in the library, but I was seen as misguided and unable to see the patient's destructiveness because of some involvement of my own which I should analyse in myself. I so hate this condescending attitude from these people. In the absence of argument they resort, basically, to 'there must be something wrong with you if you don't agree with us'. I feel so insulted by all this, and the trouble is that if I were still in analysis I would have some support. But I won't put myself back in treatment just because they cannot accept my opinion. My analysis took five years, and a year to end. I'm not going to turn all that upside down for them. Do you think I'm wrong? Do you think all this *is* me? I have never felt so bad about a case, or rather about what's happening between me and the clinic team. It would be terrible to resign only a few months after taking the post.

But the staff meetings *are* terrible and I find I can think about little else. I tried going to an art gallery. Rodin sculptures you would have thought would drive away this ugly business. Instead what was in front of me but his *Prodigal Son*, can you believe it? It could have been modelled on Sylvan! I stood there for I don't know how long, half an hour, first of all marvelling at the coincidence, it was almost as though it were planned, and then willing for it to be Sylvan, it looked so much like him, and found myself imagining him coming back. But Rodin shows only the yearning, the desperation and the longing of the boy who has cut himself off, not the return. The one clenched fist is raised higher, while the other beseeching, open hand seems to fall back. I could not properly see the rest of the exhibition, it seemed so hollow with that piece there that so much spoke of what that boy is putting himself through. And I wondered, like the *Prodigal Son*, is there some salvation that he is finding, in his own way?

Love from Helen.

(She picks up another letter.)

Dear Sylvan, I read your letter. I am very concerned that you are putting yourself in such danger. I have written to your social worker who I hope will get in touch and try and help you. You make yourself very alone if you refuse help like this. Since it is clear that you will not be continuing psychotherapy I want to suggest that you receive in-patient treatment in a therapeutic community. I would rather have discussed this with you in person . . .

(Blackout)

SYLVAN *(reads from his notebook.)*

We speak to each other in the quiet shadows
As though thousands of thousands
Have not been slaughtered,
More cruelly than nature could design.

We speak as though we were human,
As if we were not murderers,
Traitors and collaborators,
The ones who bulldozed
Heaps of corpses into the pit.

Forgetting our complicity,
No blood on our hands.

And if ever the bright flame of shame
Lights upon who we are,
We shrink and hide,
And thank our gods,
Wherever they are,
As it flickers out,
Soon enough.

(He picks up a letter.)

Dear Helen, I'm really enjoying this poetry writing. I don't mind if it's any good or not, I just love seeing something on paper. I've no idea what it means, really. It just sounds wonderful, like the poets I'm reading. And some of these French poets are saying that <u>art is the only important thing</u>.

Reading them I've found, at last, people who could understand how I've had to debase myself. Until now I've had nothing that could give me a purpose. I've found one now. I was so excited, I laughed out loud in the library when I read about something called 'the systematic disorientation of the senses'. So perhaps I could use all of this for something?

And someone called Baudelaire, I think it is, wrote,

'Yesterday I felt the wing of madness pass over me.' Wow!

Why am I writing this to you? I hope it doesn't make things difficult for you. I would spoil things after all. But perhaps you never even read this far. I find myself hoping for that.

There is something brutal about your so-called professional relationship. You can approach so far, and no further! I could never think of asking, nor even *think* of some other contact with you, someone who at last seemed to understand me. I have to stop writing to you, obviously. Your people, I am sure, are not very happy with it. I'm putting too much onto you and I'm sorry about that. It's not at all your fault and I want you to know that, whatever happens it's not your fault.

Yours, Sylvan Johnson

(Blackout)

DR HERMANN *(steps forward and speaks to audience.)*

We cannot possibly help this patient who has himself systematically rejected treatment.

All that remains now is to discharge him. It is important that you do nothing further to encourage his obsessive letter-writing. And do not be deceived by this so-called poetry, for it is nothing but a grandiose expression of his pathological preoccupations. The experience of this clinic over the years has been the value of keeping boundaries. These kinds of patients will undermine and destroy treatment unless we stick carefully to our limits, though it may feel rigid to some. He is no longer our patient.

(Blackout)

ANNA *(speaking to HELEN)*

Dear Helen, some afterthoughts from our telephone talk last night. Don't worry, I'm not going to reiterate 'you have to let it go' and all that. There were two points really that have been bothering me. One is the split that has developed between you and the rest of the team, where each side is seeing the other exactly the same way, as so misguided and unable to see the patient's needs. And in the middle of it is Sylvan himself, who does not come for treatment. In fact he has created this situation and it must be a reflection of a split in himself; the side of him that wants help, human contact, and to change, he locates in you, which you respond to, but he doesn't come to you, he stays away and shows the other side, that rejects, wallows in self-destruction. You have to realise that this is fundamentally anti-life, and this is the side of him that Mark and the clinic team pick up on. It is as if there is a good mother somewhere for him and he cannot reach her, and so he destroys the possibility of their union. This has been the story of his life, his whole identity. The male in him, that has been so abusive, is struggling to find expression and, yes, I agree he is trying creatively to heal the split in himself, and maybe he will be able to do so on his own. If not, then he is a casualty of war. There is a war going on, all the time, within human nature, and we fight it and survive it as best we can. But never mind my philosophising!

My other thought is about the choice of you as therapist. Giving a boy like him a young woman therapist was a bad decision. How could he not be attracted, even fall in love? This would be a healthy response, but in therapy it could only be seen as an ill part of himself. Intimacy in therapy sessions with you would be overwhelming to him. He would have to run away. Maybe this could not have been foreseen, but it is also possible that unconsciously the clinic does offer up a sacrificial victim to cases of abuse that it knows it cannot win. It was too easy at the beginning, a nice case for you! His background was dreadful. His current life situation was hopeless. But psychotherapy is all a clinic like that can do. A peashooter against battleships. But you don't have to be cannon fodder; you can learn how much we can do, and where we cannot help. Well, there is hope that maybe sitting there in the library, he will come to a better understanding of himself and be able to move on, and find something, or someone who does care, as much as you have, and this time be able to use what they offer him.

Love, Anna

(Blackout)

HELEN *(reads from letter.)*

Dear Anna, I have just heard from his social worker that Sylvan has died from an overdose. His body was found in his hostel bedsit. It is thought that he had been dead for almost a week. A syringe was still in his arm.

Maybe it was accidental, it's hard to say. Is there any such thing as an accident? I can't believe it was really intended because in his last letter to me it seemed that in reading and writing poetry he had discovered something that would keep him going. It also felt like he was giving up his fixation on me and moving on to something else. Maybe these were the challenges he could not face. I will have to live with not knowing. Just now I am wondering why on earth we do this work.

I have resigned from the clinic. It's not just this case.

I'm just not thinking in the same way as the clinicians here. The discussions are so competitive, with each one trying to outsmart the rest in their clever interpretations of patients' behaviour. It is increasingly obvious that I am out of step. There seems to be no concept of actually relating to a person – only the 'patient' is talked about. No wonder so many don't return. Some of these therapists just seem to sit and watch for the signs of hostility in their patients. You can hear them justify this 'rigorous technique' by their mission to focus on the destructive part of the patient's personality. So the ones who stay become enraged and full of hate at this so-called therapist who cannot relate to them emotionally. Either that or they give in and masochistically enjoy all this about their hostility and destructiveness. I was beginning to be driven mad by interpretations that begin 'you want me to . . .' or 'you fear that I . . .', 'you are angry with me because . . .' and so forth. Sylvan *should* have had someone who cared about him, a safe place to be, *should* have had a better life. Traumatised patients need assurance that someone knows this. Constantly putting back to them the ways in which they have themselves become destructive is rubbing salt into the wound. They may be addicted to self-harm, they may be undermining the treatment relationship, but someone *should have known*, and *should know NOW* what it is they have been through. All this stuff about 'projective identification', 'getting into the therapist to attack and destroy the good object' seems to be a substitute for common concern.

Mark Hermann could never acknowledge how he felt about Sylvan! We never spoke about the fact that Mark made an emotional contact with Sylvan that could not carry over to me. Nor about how he really felt at my failure to work with Sylvan. This place being seen as so special seems to make it more of an impossibility to relate in an ordinary way.

Maybe I am soft, as they say, trying to make up for the lack of love, in a futile effort to be a better parent than the patient had. I couldn't help Sylvan. And maybe it is my anger about this that makes me turn on the others as though it was their fault that I failed. Perhaps I just can't hack it at this high-powered clinic where I so much wanted to be. All I know is I cannot stand it here any more and so I'm going to an ordinary little psychiatric unit that you won't have heard of. There will be no shortage of people who need help. I can work in my own way. I don't mind if they call me by my first name.

It hasn't been a completely negative experience being here, even for such a short time. I've learned something about my limitations, about my need to be special, about protecting myself.

Love, and thanks, Helen

(Blackout)

PART III

RUTH *(holds in her hands a letter which she partly reads from and partly speaks to. She is walking about angrily addressing JOHN, who is sitting impassively in a chair. It is as if he does not hear.)*

I hate you, I hate you, I hate you.

I came out of tonight's group in a fury and despite most of a bottle of wine, I won't sleep until I get something down on paper of what I couldn't say in the group. I want to scream that I hate you! I want to fly at you with my hair on fire, claws ready to rip you apart, tear up your smug smile. You sit there like a piece of wood, I want to chop you up and set fire to you so you know what it feels like to be burning with hatred like me.

And you know why, that's what makes me mad. You know it all, you look at me. You WATCH me churning up inside and you don't care, you just wait, you're in control, you're so cold. It makes you feel better, doesn't it, to watch me suffer, to feel safe, you offer me nothing, not a friendly hand or a word of sympathy. It's like you're watching, and judging my performance – how much of this pain can I bring out, how much can I humiliate myself in front of the others? They understand as little as you do what it's like to have suffered as I have, and to have as little emotionally as I do.

To admit how lonely and abandoned I feel, that's what you want, isn't it, and to say how much I need you. I don't need you. You think I need you, I don't, I can have men just like that, I had a bloke last week. We had sex in his car, I met him at the pub. I didn't even find out his name. And in case you were wondering, it was unprotected too. You see, I can do exactly what I want with whoever I want, and I don't need you patronising me with your concern, your interpretations about my anger to you and my self-destructiveness. Trying to make you feel guilty and helpless? No, I did it because I wanted to, I felt like it and I could do it. And you couldn't stop me. You didn't even know about it, I didn't tell you in the group did I, so you couldn't know, that's how clever you are, Mr Fucking Group Therapist.

And I'm not going to come back next week. Yes, I know it's the last one before the holiday and when you asked me what would happen if I did come to the last group before the break since I always stay away, well now you know, I would become a shrieking bitch and kill every last one of the rest of the group as well. Except Annie, she cares for me. But even that you have to spoil, by commenting on how I have to make alliances to 'deny the bad mother'. Yes, I do feel attacked by Maggie, by her disapproval. She's just a bitter and twisted middle-aged woman who, because she is divorced, can have no fun, nor anything spontaneous in life ever again. No wonder her husband left her for someone younger and more fun. You'd think she might learn something from that, but no she just closes into her mask of depression. It's not a depression, it's evil, waiting to leap out and snatch at somebody who appears at all vulnerable. And can you do anything to stop her? No.

I'm staying away next week, not because I'm scared to say any of this to her or to any of the others, but because I won't give you the satisfaction of seeing me show my true feelings. Maggie knows, just as the men know what I think. They're a bunch of wimps, pathetically unable to assert themselves in any way, whining on in the group about this, or that, they can't cope with. They know I could wipe the floor with them. But you, leaving me for the whole summer, five weeks! I refuse to humiliate myself in front of you and them by saying how devastated this makes me feel.

You're relentless, you're brutal. You know I still

haven't got over David and Jenny joining the group. You've no compunction about bringing in new people next term, even though you know that when someone new comes in then I can't take part and the whole term has been wasted for me. You know how I hate to have to say who I am yet again and my background. And this is where you say I'm trying again now to be so special.

I dreamt that you held a snake in your hand and I thought, no it's not poison, it's medicine.

So are you going to throw me out of the group if I stay away? Perhaps I'm trying to get you to throw me out. You could do it and then they would all see what a bastard you really are. How could you do that, when I so obviously need to be in the group? But one thing I'd like to know. If I so much need to be in the group, how come I'm supposed to last five weeks without it? How does that fit in to your scheme? If I'm supposed to go five weeks without therapy then maybe I don't need to be in the group at all? No, the only reason it's five weeks is for your convenience isn't it, because you want to go away for that long. And to hell with the patients, or at least the one who really needs to be there, the one with real problems and who is really trying to do some work on them. The others don't object because they're not really serious.

Well I've got things to do, I have to get on with my work. But I'm stuck, I'm wasting my time working in the gallery, not producing my own work. I'm floating, drifting.

I was working on a three-dimensional collage of a swimming pool. Deep blue water, with red patches and bits of bodies, limbs, necks, torsos, no faces or heads. But with what materials, I couldn't decide.

Perhaps the idea is too close to the bone, ha ha. Too close to my feelings anyway about my family. I have to try and get past these ghosts, get on to something else, yes, just as you say, I should stop, but how to break free of the past? I know you think so badly of me because of the affair with Ian, but you judge me too harshly. It's all I have, it has to be secret and I know I'm doing the same as I always did, keeping secrets, but if I've got nothing else for the summer break, how can I do without that?

What's the alternative? Loneliness. Having no one is just so awful for me.

You say something prevents me from having an open and honest relationship, but where is it? OK, I can pick up a bloke in the pub, but neither he nor I are interested in more than a night together. I don't think I even particularly liked the look of him. There just aren't any nice men who are going to look after me. Not any who would look at me anyway. This is the bitter pill that you make me swallow. There is no one who is going to look after me!

So back to work in my empty studio. Perhaps I can put some of this into my work? Could you understand what I've made? You won't even come to see it. I don't believe your reasons. I think you just don't want to, do you? Or scared? Afraid I would have some power over you, might bite you?

But no, I just want to make something clean, so fine it has nothing to do with me. It would be completely separate, no one would be able to tell whose it was or that the person who made it was a victim, whose mother committed suicide and brother died at 18, in other words who came from a totally fucked up family. Something to take me above all that.

And then I know what you would say, to get that I would have to bring all the hatred and abuse to the group, and then my mind and my work would be free of it.

Does it mean I have to go in this group forever? Maybe I do. I can't imagine leaving. And that's why I can't bear to come next week because there is something from the group I can't get anywhere else. My past will never change, no matter how hard I work or what I do.

I'm sorry about the beginning of this letter, but I will send it anyway, because it is still part of everything. Now I've got it out of my system, I probably will come along next week. You win.

Love, NO love from Ruth Johnson

JOHN *(he speaks directly to audience)*

Ruth has been probably my most difficult patient; she has the ability to unsettle me, to get under my skin. Nothing I can say is right! She's attention-seeking, angry, she monopolises the group, is hostile to the others, challenging me constantly . . . but she's also enlivening, she dares to say the things that others might only think.

(Nervously)

She is attractive; she has a certain sexual power. I like her, but I have to be very careful about how I respond because

(somewhat primly)

I don't want her to think that she can seduce me.

(More professionally)

I'm very aware of her history of losses and child sexual abuse. I have to be quite strict with myself, but she complains I am strict with her. She talks provocatively about her affairs and sexual encounters, and I take up her need to have someone – me – to keep her safe (as if I could!). I say we have to find out why she is so self-destructive, but whatever I say seems to infuriate her. She says I don't understand her feelings, she can't rely on me, she can't share me with the others, she can't stand me talking to anyone other than her. She insists she needs my one-to-one attention.

Well, maybe she would be better off in individual treatment, not with me, that wouldn't feel right (perhaps I don't trust myself?), but she refuses to go to anyone else. And anyway, she says, she had individual therapy before, which was right for her at the time, she had a breakdown in adolescence, and she doesn't want to go back to that. For a long time we've been stuck.

Maybe I should stop trying to be the professional and think for a moment what is happening to me. Am I flattered to be so important that she needs me and cannot bear to see anyone else? But it's not very nice to be made to feel so completely useless. Of course, it's to do with her background, she never had a real parent. She can't believe that she won't be dropped again. And then there is the incestuous relationship with her brother, closeness and intimacy for her have become sexualised. But the more I try to convey that this is different, that I'm offering her something else, the more I seem to fail her. I'm nothing, compared to the family members in her head. Although dead, they are more real to her than I am. And the group is just a series of puppets, dummies, or dolls she uses to convey her projections. Not only am I useless, but it's all worthless, she's managing to destroy my group!

Sometimes, I have to admit, I want her to just go away (I'm careful not to communicate that, of course), but she's quite frankly a bloody nuisance. She taunts me with her sexuality. She talks about an affair with a married man, amazing sexual experiences, trying to make others envious, excited and excluded, instead of her feeling those things, all of which I've interpreted – but then we hear that his wife has taken an overdose and nearly died. She was distressed about this, and got the sympathy of the group, the women at least, but I felt they were all in a crazy distortion of reality, as though it was the woman's fault, the one who took the overdose ('what a terrible thing to do!'), and that Ruth bore no responsibility. I thought that there was also something here about her denial of guilt feelings for her mother's suicide. I said something like this and she flew off the handle. 'There you are,' she said to the others, 'he kicks me when I'm down, he twists the knife in!' I kept quiet then, and she found support from the others, but I was getting the message here, that someone has to die; either it's the wife of a man Ruth is having it off with, or me annihilated as a therapist, or Ruth herself feeling destroyed. The trouble is that I can see, exactly see, how a married man could be turned on by her; she is exciting because she doesn't care. She's so intense, I feel weak next to her, and it is a delicious weakness, it makes me think of her body and being overwhelmed by her. But that would be suicide, professionally. And in fact I have had thoughts at times; I imagined crashing my car, what a relief! But the week would roll around and there she'd be again. There seemed no escape. So perhaps there was a certain satisfaction when I could point this out to her, like with the wife's suicide attempt, you bad girl, look at what happens when you misbehave! I was trying to control her instead of myself. Being 'the therapist' was a way for me to hide my true feelings.

It is almost as if I am the brother driven to self-destruct because he cannot have her, or even the mother who cannot cope with her, and throws it all in. If I'm not keeping control, I become them. So I have wondered, well what if it's true? Instead of fighting this, let's say that I am the brother who can't ever fulfil his desire, or the mother who can neither love her nor let go. How would I feel if I were either of them? If I were to say to myself, I'll never have her, well then, I'd just be tremendously sad about that. And after all the fury and refusal to accept this, I'm left with an emptiness, a space; and yet she hasn't gone away, she is going to come back next week – how strange, now I find myself glad of this. If I stop fighting my own loss of her, if I see really that I'll never have her, never own her, but that she would still be there, at least it eases the pressure. Maybe I really can give her nothing, no love from me, but I would be there too, and listen to what comes next.

So I felt braver when she said the following week how she could never forgive me the things I said. I answered yes, it's unforgivable that I am not the one to take away the hurt from the losses you have had. And it hurts more that all I do is bring about more and more loss. Someone else in the group said that he thought I was talking as much about myself as about her.

RUTH *(She finishes a letter and reads it out, speaking partly to the audience.)*

I've seen my mother's letter, her suicide note, addressed as it was, to her social worker, not to me, or my brother. I went along and asked for information about her. It was several months before they decided I could see it, and what a palaver I had to go through to persuade them! My being in therapy seemed to make a difference. They allowed me to make a copy of the letter and I think I'll give you a copy. And just now I have to get it, right at the bloody summer break again. It always seems to come at the wrong time!

I've read it about ten times. And I'll probably need to read it another ten. It's told me such a lot, made so much sense of many things. But I always end up feeling so sad for her, at times angry with her but then so sorry. And what the death of her mother must have meant for her! It's not the hatred I used to feel for her. That's gone now. I don't know if it will stop the hatred I sometimes feel for you, though! But you kept me on with my idea to get information from the social services about my past even when I thought it would be pointless. It has also changed my view about my brother and I can see how he used sex to get close. How rejected he must have felt when it all came out. We had been close for a good few years after mum died. When we were fostered or in children's homes we clung together for protection. That must have been how the sex started. Sleeping together for comfort became something else for him. Then it was something else for me. This has always been difficult for me to say in the group. You have to understand sometimes I was battling for your attention because there were things I really felt I couldn't say in front of the others. How would they understand? Maybe jealousy as well and my need to be special as you would always say, but you know, people don't really talk about sexual feelings in our group, maybe they're too scary. Scary for me, anyway.

I used to pretend to be asleep. I would leave the covers off me. I'd throw my arm against him, or open my legs with my eyes closed, pretending it wasn't really me doing it. Sometimes he would just sit there on the edge of the bed, and I'd feel the bed shaking. I felt sorry for him then as well, though I think I felt powerful over him in a secret way. That's been my power over men, something else you've been on about as well, as they can get so excited over me, but always the question when am *I* going to get my pleasure? Something else instead of the feeling of power over them. And I've realised that power is what I feel WHEN I'M SEEN.

But then he would force his way into me. Always very hasty and furtive for fear of being discovered. He must have been just as scared as I was. Always something missing, the essential thing not there. Mum's letter explained this to me when she spoke about her lover's body, those were exactly the feelings that I wanted to have for myself. I wanted to be that perfect white body, so loved for itself. And I've never felt that way about myself before, but I've always wanted to. Instead I've always felt the victim. I've never felt I could be the active one you see. Oh yes, active by seducing, as you keep saying, I'm good at that. And that's how I get back at my brother, all the time. But it's as though my eyes are closed all the time. What's woken up in me now is that I want to make love with my eyes open. I want to see the shape of my lover. I want my own shape. Like my mother wanted hers. She's gone now, but with that letter, with being so present to me through it, strangely enough now I feel she really has gone. I think I've at last really met her so that now she can really leave.

I think of her lying in that room for days and days, tracing the outline of her life and finding that it was over. I can still feel my old resentment against her for not struggling on for our sake, but for her the fight was over, she could do no more. And I've lain in my bed for hours on my own. When I do so now, I feel a little bit at one with her. I try to comfort her. I can say to her that she did give me life. And I can make something, make a shape out of this life she gave me. Does this sound crazy, but the bits of work I've done I now can see have been my feeble attempts to make something out of what she gave me. Through the painting I was working on, of a house with no doors or windows, only writing on the outside walls, my writing about the abuse, I was trying to convey that I was trapped inside. But how can anyone know if they don't know what it is that they see? Does art have an audience? Writing has readers, music has listeners, art has what? Watchers? What are they thinking, what are you thinking, I'll never know. I was asking someone to at least be aware of the closed up house of my existence, my coffin. And the big metal claw, I can now see as my mother who was reaching out to me in a cold and terrifying way, but it wasn't really her, only what I imagined was her.

I have a lot of work to do this summer. I have lots of ideas for new work. Having time now is suddenly an enormous luxury. How quickly it passes when I'm working and how slowly when I'm breaking apart.

I'm thinking about a new piece, a smooth long shape and am preparing myself to make it. It will be black, infinitely smooth, made out of marble. About four feet by eighteen inches or so with a groove down the middle. It is a sort of body, or part of one, a part suggesting the whole. But it is, or will be, what it is, in the same way as I am what I am now, not something or someone trying to be other. My images now are of wholeness. I have you to thank for some of this. If I'd seen my mother's letter before I'd have been crushed, I think, by the awful brutality of the facts. The group and you have made me stronger. I feel so much better that I've given up the affair with Ian. Perhaps it took his wife's overdose to wake me up to what I was doing. But I couldn't have done it on my own. I've been amazed by Jenny's and Annie's acceptance of me, no matter how bad I can be, even David's admiration (ha!) that continues even after I've been a bitch to him and you, your tolerance despite my vileness to you. I even feel something for the other men in the group. We're in the same boat in a way. All this has made me believe I can be a person after all – Before you knew me a long time ago, I had a phobia of showing my face, literally I used to hide my face all the time.

Cynthia helped me with that, she released me from the guilt I had about sex with my brother, thinking that I had caused the death of my mother.

– When you released the butterfly in the last session I burst into tears and couldn't explain why. It was trapped between the window panes and you said, just open the window, don't touch the butterfly because if you touch the wings it won't be able to fly, just open the window and wait until it decides to leave. The group carried on and as you noticed, I couldn't take part. You said to me, it is difficult to let the butterfly go in its own time. And as you said that it dropped down between the sash windows and flew out. I was speechless and you said that it was something to do with the summer break, and I'm sorry that I just couldn't take it, I felt so ashamed, I couldn't say that it wasn't just going away for August, it's the going away I have to do, every time, now, and in the future, for ever, leaving you, and knowing that I will never be really close, as close as I want, and be really looked after by you, that you will always let me go, and not even touch me, for fear that I would not be able to fly away, or be myself, I suppose.

I know I have to be myself and go away, but it's so hard, I want to stay. I'm going to hate myself for having said all this, for having revealed myself. I want you to pretend in the group that you haven't read any of this. But you won't, I know. You always push me away, even though you know how painful it is for me. I still hate you, but it's no good is it, to go on hating. There comes a point when I have to go on, go away and I'm crying as I write this because I can't be with you. I have no right to ask so much. Only a little, and then no more! I want to cry out that it is too little, but I don't, I behave properly, mostly. Just as long as you know, and the rest of them, I don't mind, they have to know and it's all right. After all it's all right.

See you in September.

Signed, Ruth

(Blackout)

Author's Note

A play about psychotherapy, about adolescence, abuse, drug addiction, suicide and failed treatment may well have seemed an unlikely project, perhaps more a recipe for disaster! But I started writing with no clear aim in mind. Originally I think I was giving vent to feelings and thoughts about cases (people whom I was trying to help) and staff group dynamics (situations with people I was supposed to be working with). In fact the experiences were a general mix of therapeutic 'failures' and professional (near) disasters. Because they were 'impossible' situations, full of unknowns, and subject to any number of interpretations, I felt free to imagine stories and the characters. The fictional form of letter writing appealed because there was a greater range to the imagination; I could perhaps say things that would otherwise be unacceptable. I did not anticipate that the characters would soon develop what seemed like their own voices. At the time of writing I vaguely thought that a series of letters might tie together well enough to make something like a novel. But when I showed some early drafts to one or two people, they thought it could work dramatically. And so I shaped the piece in that direction.

The text has had two parallel forms of existence: it has been used in workshops for professionals and/or trainees who are thinking about the personal impact of their work with clients or patients, and also in performances for an audience. In these latter projects I have been tremendously encouraged by friends and colleagues. Sally Willis, a fellow group analyst with a background in the theatre, took it on with her friend Cindy Grenville and recruited a cast, consisting first of all of amateurs, who gradually gave way to those with a training. I am particularly indebted to Bryan Boswood for fostering that first stage. Ann Alvarez gave it a place at a Conference at the Tavistock Centre in November 1999. Five further performances have ensued, and more are planned. But despite the confidence of others, each time the event drew nearer I have been almost overwhelmed by anxieties approaching the level of sheer terror. My worries about disapproval, ridicule, embarrassment, rejection, have turned into a rising panic as I realise how much of myself I might have exposed, unintentionally, in these stories. But now as I see the piece again or hear it being discussed, I marvel at something being brought to life. And as with living things, new connections emerge, different aspects unfold that I had not envisaged before. I wonder at how it all came from somewhere that was both *me* and *not me*, from something that cannot really be called *my* unconscious. As I have been reassured (as well as amazed) at the positive responses it has received, I have also begun to feel somewhat detached, and separate. It is as though the piece has a life of its own, and has become a sort of magic formula that has a power to call up those characters, people who are like old friends, from another part of my life.

Who is who?

As I did not start out to produce a play, it is not surprising that the text is not exactly a drama. The characters do not speak to each other so much as use each other to find their own voice. The process started with a particular adolescent in my mind who wanted to be heard, but (as often happens with young people in treatment) cannot bear anyone to listen. He came to represent not only the young people I may have failed, but also the failed young man I could have been. Poems came to mind that seemed

from him, not me. Here was a different version of myself.
Since I was not really that self-destructive young person,
I had to think what would have happened to have made
me so. What would his mother have been? As she too
became real her voice became clearer and I knew then
that she had killed herself, and was still consumed with
anger. That was the anger and the protest that echoed
down the years and were burning up this boy. For a time
I found myself dreaming what seemed to be her dreams.
Thus she in turn became another inner voice, another
self-possibility. She was not *my* mother, but (again) could
have been. I have been asked whether John, the group
therapist, is actually me, or is Sylvan really Woods?
Helen, the junior therapist, undergoes an initiation into
malignant staff group dynamics very similar to my own
experiences a few years ago and pays the price of becoming a therapist. But I also had great sympathy with Dr
Hermann, who takes the role of villain. He has the courage to say the necessary 'No'. So when Nancy Brenner
of the Anna Freud Centre said that she could hear my
voice in all the characters, even though each was believ-
ably different, I felt I had received a compliment, but I
was also intrigued; if they are all aspects of myself, what
am I doing using my patients' material, and even imagining their lives, in this way?

Working with art and working with patients

After one performance I looked at Joyce McDougall's *Many Faces of Eros*. She says that 'there is always a risk that a creative act will be experienced unconsciously as a crime against the parents' . . . because . . . 'one must assume the right to be both fertile womb, and the fertilizing penis' (McDougall, 1977: 101). Sylvan, my adolescent character proclaims art as 'the only important thing'. He is using his creativity as an alternative to reality. Poetry is an area of omnipotence for him, and he rejoices that he does not know what it means, i.e., that he has no responsibility to relate it to the reality of the rest of his life. Coming from a family of artists I know that art is far from automatically good and healthy. It is characteristic of adolescence to try things out, to test limits, to seek outlandish experiences, and then after a while, to work them through in something like psychotherapy. In my story, however, Sylvan's creativity draws upon his hatred of the parents, and his self-hatred, and he is left without a safe haven. Thus he turns away from help.

As a psychotherapist I sometimes feel torn between science and art. A practitioner is expected to work within the limits of observable phenomena and measurable results, but I also believe that there are certain aspects of psychotherapy that are only accessible through creative means. The effectiveness of treatment may depend on indefinable qualities, such as the capacity for empathy, or the ability of a therapist to be guided by their own internal process. Therapists are brought up against their wishful thinking, subjectivity, and omnipotent solutions to the clash between fantasy and reality. But art, as an alternative route, also cannot exist in a solipsistic universe. If it is to communicate (and is it worth anything if it does not communicate?) it has to be about a struggle with reality.

In her Foreword, Estela Welldon has described an experience coincidentally similar to an episode from *The End of Abuse*. She had been agonising over a difficult case, an assessment report of a young mother for the Court. She visited an art gallery and saw a Giacometti that perfectly expressed the emptiness at the core of a maternal relationship. Then, said Estela, she knew what it was she was seeing in the clinical work. In my story the junior therapist, Helen, preoccupied with her feelings about Sylvan, sees Rodin's *The Prodigal Son*; her hopes are sustained that in some way her patient, will, after all, find salvation. In these events there seems to have been a moment when the therapist steps back emotionally, detaches herself somewhat and looks at her own experience from a new angle. By doing this she finds a communication which is both from outside and within her own world, a perception of art that makes sense of both the separation *and* the involvement. This aesthetic experience, it seems to me, shows that therapist and patient are the same, and are also different; the privileged self of 'therapist' gives way momentarily, to an inner experience for the therapist of the underprivileged self we call 'patient'.

Individual and group; the psychic and the social

My story ends with Ruth, a child no longer, struggling with her rage against the therapist. At last it seemed that the protests could be heard, in the arena of a group. I have been asked if I believe only in group therapy. No, like much else in the text, it just seemed right. I felt at that time that writing about individual therapy was going to be more difficult and I was putting it off until a later date. But the group also came to mind I think because it represented, as it does now, my own need of the family, friends, colleagues, and the 'therapeutic community' of other workers in the field, who have sustained me. No psychotherapist can go on indefinitely, even with purely 'individual' work, without regular recourse to his or her group, of whatever description. Throughout the process of this play, in productions and workshops, an organised depiction of my inner chaos, both personally and professional, has been made real and comprehensible by a group, a complexity of several groups, too numerous to mention here. These real groups seem to have nurtured the neglected children and parents of my imagination. In the final letter Ruth accepts that she cannot have the therapist to herself, and so is released from the traumatic loss of her mother. For this to happen there had to be, paradoxically, a tolerable degree of abuse and exploitation in the therapeutic process. What I felt I was witnessing as it came to me in this story, was that which had been so difficult in the characters' lives, a healthy separation and growth, an adolescent blossoming at last.